Acknowle

My grateful thanks go to Tao ?
the illustrations free of charge.

To Viv and Myra Emerson and Kathy Munns who
painstakingly proof-read all I wrote.

To Rev. David Shaw and the Reading and Silchester
Methodist Circuit
The Southampton Methodist District and
Caversham Heights Methodist Church for helping to finance
the project.

To Brenda Caborn for working so hard on the publicity and
press releases.

Also my thanks go to the many people who have helped and
encouraged me in thought, word and prayer throughout the
whole venture.

# Contents            Pages

# In the shadows of victory:
## ride the rollercoaster of Holy Week

by
Becky Lovatt

First published November 2013

Printed by:

www.direct-pod.com

Illustrations © Tao Barry DipSBA

ISBN 978-1-909424-65-4

Dedicated to: Tim, Emerald and Theo

All proceeds from the sale of this book will go to
Buscot Ward—the Special Care Unit at the
Royal Berkshire Hospital in Reading.

It is with many thanks that I dedicate this book to the staff who
offered care and support when we lost our daughter Emerald
and who looked after my son Theo and me in the early days of
his life.

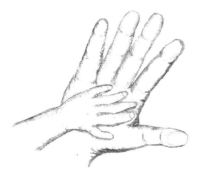

> *Trust in the LORD with all your heart, and do not rely on your own
> insight. In all your ways acknowledge him, and he will make
> straight your paths.*
>
> *Proverbs 3:5-6*

# Contents                                                        Pages

# Palm
# Sunday

## Dangerous Day

We now begin the journey, remembering that already we stand with Jesus Christ our Saviour in the shadow of the cross, remembering that for him, it was a very dangerous day.

Jesus knew exactly what he was doing mounting the donkey at Bethpage, as this was where the priests had calculated the city limits. For Jesus to mount here was a statement that spoke volumes to all that were there. It was, in effect, as if He was shouting from the rooftops that He was the Messiah.

Now, position yourself at the side of the road, having first run and chopped down a palm branch that you are waving frantically.

Picture if you can the Roman army standing there, thousands of them, making it very clear that you are part of an occupied people. Look up at the temple on the hill, and look beyond it. There overshadowing the holy place is the fist shaped Roman fortress. Built purposely taller than the temple just to remind you who was in charge.

Listen to the crowd hailing him as their King. But He does not come on a war horse, only a humble donkey. And He does not come with swords and clubs; He is armed only with God's words of peace and love.

Wave your branches, as they are the national symbol of your people. Wave them at the coming Messiah, showing your defiance to the Romans, believing that this Jesus would send them packing once and for all.

Jesus knew that for Him, it was a very dangerous day.

Picture the children laughing and playing around your feet. In your fear, you push them forward. Somehow this fear is always lurking beneath your joy; your fear of the Roman soldiers and the power they hold over you. The children - they are young, surely these soldiers wouldn't launch an attack against them, no matter how unruly the crowd become. Push them forward, put them between you and the soldiers, not because you do not love your children, but because you fear for your own safety.

Jesus knew that for Him, it was a very dangerous day.

Sing your hosannas, not just a song of happiness, but also a song of rebellion, a song that speaks of freedom, and of victory over your enemies. Stand tall in the face of those who persecute you. Hold firm, ready to take up arms and fight, ready to rally around this new king and take back, by force if you have to, your land, and your home.

Jesus knew that for Him, it was a very dangerous day.

## Pause for thought:

- How do you reflect on Jesus' dangerous day?

- In our dangerous days how might we react and what lessons might we draw from the example of Jesus?

# For thirty pieces of silver
## The voice of Judas.

My name is Judas Iscariot and it is a name that will be remembered for centuries to come. I was there, you see, following Him, I was there when the crowds hailed Him as king and He made His triumphal entry into Jerusalem on the back of a donkey - let me tell you all about it.

We had spent three years playing at it, living as occupied people in an occupied land. The Romans dominated everything; we lived under their rule, but secretly we dreamed of regaining our homeland.

I joined a small group of freedom fighters, but our numbers were few, our weapons were fewer, and before long our enthusiasm began to fade. But then, about three years ago He arrived - Jesus of Nazareth. A carpenter by trade but He could really tell a story.

Somehow, He spoke with authority, crowds gathered around like bees to a honey pot, and they hung on his every word. Hope began to rekindle; maybe this was the man who would call us to arms, form us into an army, and reclaim our land, by force if we had to.

However, He had preached love and kindness, He had rebuked scribes and priests, He had eaten with tax collectors and sinners and healed on the Sabbath. I was beginning to doubt His qualifications, maybe He wasn't the revolutionary I had hoped for after all.

But then... then I was surprised, as He turned His face towards Jerusalem, the city of our God and centre of our homeland. On the day we entered the city, the streets were lined with people, waving palms, shouting Hosannas and hailing Him as king. And I was there too; part of the throng, maybe it would happen after all, maybe this was the beginning.

The Romans looked on, spears in hand, just to make sure that the crowd did not overstep the mark. And He, He rode a donkey, not a white horse, like a king, or a war horse like an army general, but a donkey, plain and simple, placid and peaceful, what did this say?

I walked into the city with mixed feeling; half of me was full of excitement, maybe this was it - the beginning of the end for our oppressors. The other half was full of anger; perhaps revolution on my terms was not what Jesus planned.

<u>Pause for thought:</u>

- What are your thoughts about Judas' disappointment?

- How might you have felt if you were there?

# You should have seen it
## The voice of Lucca

Wow what a day!!
You should have seen it!!!

I was minding my own business on the way to the city for the Passover festival when I was caught up in the commotion.

Crowds and crowds of people.
All shouting and waving coats and palms, anything they could get hold of really.

There were children singing,
Excited women,
And men visibly growing in stature, ready to stand up and fight for what was rightfully theirs.

The soldiers were on high alert.
The priests were clearly concerned and unsure.
And the people He brought with Him were loyal and obedient, ready to follow at any cost, and hanging on His every word.

And there He was.
People called him Jesus,
The Lamb of God,
The Son of David,
Even, the Messiah, the chosen one of God.

They believed He would raise an army,
So they hailed Him as king.

They thought He would bring freedom
So they pledged themselves to Him and to His service.

But I did not see a warlord.
I did not see jewels in a crown,
Or an army marching with swords and clubs.
Nor did I hear words of uprising,
Or any call to arms.

Instead I saw a man, humbly riding on a donkey and speaking love.

I, like everyone else, was glad to be a part of it.
I knew this was the start of something big.
I could sense that this man drew people to Him
And I felt that He had the power to change those around Him.

And He did!!!


## Pause for thought:

- How might our lives be changed by Jesus?

- How might we express that change to others?

## I was out to keep the peace
## The voice of a Roman Soldier

It was just another working day for me and the team. I was head of about twenty men, all assigned to the streets of Jerusalem. We'd had our orders, to be a presence, to keep the peace, and to demonstrate the power of Rome. All was going according to plan, or so we thought. The morning had passed uneventfully, but we did not know or anticipate what was coming next.

As the afternoon wore on, more and more people began to gather. A large gathering of people always made me nervous.

Before long, there were thousands, all shouting and singing some kind of hymn of praise. Hosanna, I think it was, it meant nothing to me. My men started to twitch, they were getting very worried about the situation, and if I am honest so was I.

Rome was the dominant force, and we the Roman soldiers held court, we were quick to stamp on trouble makers, and we were not renowned for showing mercy. Normally the people of Israel knew their place; they kept quiet and did as they were told.

But that day was different. That day, when He rode into the city on the back of a donkey, that day, they were animated. They ran in packs, cutting off palm branches and laying them at His feet. They stood defiantly against us and they had never done that before either.

It shook us to the very core. We were ready to fight, our swords were drawn and we were on high alert.

But there was not any trouble. No knives or clubs were used, no stones or sticks thrown, not even spoken words of hatred.

Just Him.

A quiet, peace-filled man. A Jew, unassuming, almost unprepared for the welcome He received. He took everything in; the crowd, hailing Him as their king, and the priests watching Him with suspicion. They knew of the reputation that followed Him and we, standing guard, were only too willing to use the power we wielded over Him.

That day, and the events that followed, made me see Rome in a different light, made me see Him with new eyes. I had thought it from the very beginning, but by its end I knew He was different, and I knew I wanted to know more about this man they called Jesus—the king of the Jews.

### Pause for thought:

- Thinking about the power that the Romans held over the Jewish nation, are there people that hold power over us?

- If so how do we react and deal with them?

- Do we hold power over others?

- If so, how do we use that power?

# Holy Monday

# I was doing a good trade
## The voice of a market trader

I was minding my own business.
I was doing a good trade, until He came along and ruined everything.

I remember it was Monday - I remember because it was the day after all the commotion in the street. The day He arrived on His donkey and turned everything on its head.

I had set out my stall as usual, with all the livestock, ready and looking its best. Birds caged, large animals tied neatly at the side, all was ready for a profitable day. I had everything from small pigeons to larger beasts, something to fit any budget. I was charging reasonable prices, you know, enough to cover my overheads, with a little profit left for me. Well, I guess it was more than a little profit, but what is a few coins between friends?

I had acquired a good pitch, just inside the main temple court. Loads of passing trade, from the very poor to the very rich, all on their way to offer a sacrifice to God.

Mugs game, if you ask me, but I guess you're not asking me, so I will get on with the story.

Anyway there I was, doing a roaring trade, when up comes Jesus.

He was really mad, almost spitting feathers. I had not seen someone that angry in a long time. He came into the courtyard and one by one turned over all the stalls. Animals, food and money went flying. It was a real mess.

His face was red with fury - He picked up a whip, untied the goats and the bigger livestock and drove them outside the temple gates. He opened the cages and waved the birds to freedom.

He shouted something about His Father's house being turned into a den of thieves. I was quite insulted, I was no thief, I was only trying to make a living.

Eventually His friends pulled him away, telling Him to stay quiet and not make a scene. Of course it was too late for that.

It didn't surprise me that He was later arrested and crucified, you could see He was a trouble maker. Thank goodness I say.

<u>Pause for thought:</u>

- Jesus displayed righteous anger; are there times and situations when it is appropriate for us to do the same?

- Reflect on a time when you might have displayed righteous anger.

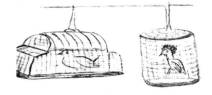

## Cleansed Demons
## The voice of Timothy

It was a Monday, and I had gone to the temple to offer praises and to worship God. I was dressed to impress, wearing my best bib and tucker, well you do, don't you, when you go to the temple? I wanted people to know that I took this God stuff seriously and of course I wanted to be seen looking my best.

I walked in through the large oak doors, past a group of women and some lepers who were not fit to enter. I didn't even acknowledge them, not even a tip of my hat or half a smile.

I took my seat, three rows from the front, with a good view of the proceedings, but not too close just in case I was asked to make a commitment to something or other. Well, you don't want to do that, do you?

All was still and quiet, but then something changed. Something new had begun and I was desperate to be a part of it. Maybe not at first, but as time went on and as order turned to chaos, I did not want to be sitting three rows back any more, I wanted to be at the front. But wait, I am getting ahead of myself, let's go back a bit.

As I have said, there I was minding my own business when there was a commotion at the door. I strained my neck to see what was going on, and then I saw Him, a man, youngish, plain looking, nothing to write home about really. He was normal, like me, but not as well dressed of course. But He was surrounded by people. Everyone wanted a piece of Him. What was He saying that was so important? Who was He anyway?

Eventually people settled, and the young man stood up. He took the scroll, read from it, handed it to the attendant and sat down. There was a hush of expectation, no-one hardly dared breathe and then He spoke. It was like nothing I had ever heard before.

His voice was soothing, interesting, meaningful, and He talked about God in a new way. In a way that somehow made God accessible, made Him more real, made Him interesting. Everyone was hanging on His every word, including me. What was it about Him, what power did He have? What authority? What hope?

But then the spell was broken. There was another noise from the door, but this time it was not a welcome one. There was a man, scruffy and unkempt, loud and unruly, who staggered into the middle of the temple. He pointed accusingly at the young man and moved towards Him threateningly. Officials from all sides stood and moved quickly towards them, ready to intervene. But wait - a silence, a calm hand in the air, like a slow motion picture, a smile, a few words and then stillness.

I watched the scruffy man, the one who had not been wanted, the one who didn't fit in, the one who stood out, and I waited. He rolled on the floor as if in great pain, he made a scene; he behaved in an inappropriate way and yet Jesus walked over, bent down and helped him up.

The man was no longer shouting, or wagging an accusing finger, he was calm, like he was somehow a new person. Suddenly he was clean and whole.

What had happened that day? How did this young travelling preacher change a man? A man in need, and a man in a bad place, a man who came into the temple searching for peace, but was only met with our disdain. A man unclean, and yet Jesus met him and cared for him. Healed him. Changed him. Loved him. And if I am honest I was changed too. I too wanted to be changed, wanted to be new, wanted to start again, hope again, live again. And Jesus, well He made all this possible.

### Pause for thought:

• How might we react if someone who is considered an outcast comes into our place of worship?

# Holy
# Tuesday

# I was blind but now I can see
## The voice of Bartimaeus

Nothing has ever been the same since that day. Well, how could it be? My whole life changed in an instant.

I was a beggar, now I am not; I was despised and rejected, now I have a place in society; and I was blind but now I can see.

My name is Bartimaeus, and I was born blind. There was much debate at the time as to whose fault that was, mine or my parents or even their parents. Something to do with the sins of the father I think, I didn't much know or care. All I know is that I was blind, but Jesus made me see.

It was a day like any other. I was up early and out on the road, I needed to get a good spot, needed to get money to feed the family, and there is not much else for a blind man to do, so begging it was.

To begin with all I heard was the everyday chatter of the street, and the sound of a few coins being tossed into my plate. But gradually I could sense the excitement rising in everyone. The noise increased and I could feel a rush of activity all around me.

What was it?

What was going on?

"Jesus is coming," someone shouted at last.

Jesus the teacher, prophet and healer. Jesus, I had heard of Him - His reputation was going before him, that was for sure.

I knew I wanted to talk with Him. Maybe He could heal me, I had thought optimistically.

I shouted too, "Jesus, Son of David, have mercy on me!" The crowd laughed at me and told me to keep quiet, not to bother the teacher. Why would He want to talk to you anyway, they said. I shouted louder, "Jesus, pity me!"

Suddenly, someone was whispering in my ear and helping me to my feet. "Hush, He is calling you." I stopped, His hand touched my shoulder and He asked, "What do you want me to do for you?"

What a dumb question, I thought, but it wasn't. He knew what He was saying, and He wanted to know that I had weighed up my answer.

I paused. "I want to see," I said.

"Then go," He told me, "Wash in the stream and see, your faith has healed you."

So I went, and washed, and just as He said I would, I could see. A whole inquisition followed, questions from priests and the crowd alike. Questions for me, my parents and my whole family. Questions, for most of which I didn't know the answer. All I could tell them was that I was blind, Jesus touched me, and now I can see.

### Pause for thought:

- Bartimaeus was physically blind, are we sometimes spiritually blind?

- Will we allow Jesus to heal us?

- When Jesus asks us, "What do you want me to do for you?", what might we say?

## Invitation to tea
## The voice of Zacchaeus the tax collector.

My name is Zaccheaus, Zac for short, and you may have heard of me. I'm the one who is short and climbed a tree to see Jesus, only for Him to invite himself to my house for tea.

It was long ago, and I am old now, but I look back with fondness, with horror and with disgust at the man I used to be. At the man I was, before Jesus changed me, before I was set free, and forgiven.

I was a very wealthy man, I still am, if you compare me with those around me that have nothing. But I share my wealth now, and use it for good, unlike before. In those days, I cooked the books, believed in creative accounting, which basically meant I got richer and every one else became poorer. I lied and cheated, and behaved appallingly, but all this did not stop Jesus from calling my name, and although I was a sinner He called me friend.

I remember the day as if it were yesterday. The streets were lined at every corner, with crowds of excited people. Jesus was coming to town. I knew of this Jesus, by reputation anyway, you could not have lived in Jericho at that time, and not have heard of Him. I wanted to see what all the fuss was about, I wanted to know if He deserved such a reputation, I needed to see for myself.

However, therein lay the problem. I was so short I couldn't see anything, only the armpits of the person in front of me. Suddenly, I had a cunning plan. I ran along the road and climbed a sycamore tree. This was perfect, I thought, I can see Him, but He can't see me.

How wrong was I?

Not long after I had settled myself down, I was disturbed.

Someone was calling my name. At first, I stayed quiet, I hoped I would blend in with the leaves. I was not a popular guy, so I prayed that the person that had spoken had mixed me up with someone else and that they would soon move on. But the calling persisted.

Who was it that called, and what did they want?

Eventually, as the crowds gathered at the foot of my tree, and the discontented mutterings increased, I realised that it was Jesus who was talking to me, and not just talking, but inviting Himself to tea.

I climbed down, and as I opened the door of my house I realised that the door of my heart had been prised open too. This man knew all about me, He saw through my lies and exposed my cheating. He never condemned me, it was I who condemned myself, because in the light of his goodness my evil was laid bare.

He called me a son of Abraham, as He offered me forgiveness. I in turn gave half of my possessions to the poor, and paid back three-fold those whom I had cheated.

He told me that salvation had come. I didn't know what that was, but I knew things could never be the same, and they never have been.

### Pause for thought:

- In the light of Christ's goodness, are there areas of our lives that appear dark, and in need of forgiveness?

# Holy
# Wednesday

## I dried my tears with my hair
## The voice of a sinful woman

Everyone considered me an outcast, and they made jolly sure I knew my place, firmly at the bottom of the pile.

Firstly, it was because I was a woman, on a sticky wicket to begin with. Secondly, it was because I had been branded a sinner. I confess, I had not followed all their rules, and gone along with their agenda, but I had to eat, and so I found whatever method I could to allow that to happen.

I had heard about Jesus. People said that He befriended sinners, ate with them, and treated people like me as His equals, giving them the opportunity to ask for forgiveness and maybe even a new start. I wanted that - I didn't want to carry on with life as it was. I wanted a fresh dawn, and I believed He could give it to me.

I knew that His friends would not allow me anywhere near Him, so I kept my ears to the ground and waited for a good time.

I heard about a dinner being hosted by one of the locals, so I turned up on the doorstep and got myself in. Officials tried to stop me, but I so wanted to see Jesus, I just kept on walking until I reached the main hall.

Suddenly, there He was, reclining at a table with the other guests. I didn't wait - I ran, hit my knees, and poured perfume from the jar I carried all over his feet.

As I did I began to cry, as the weight of all my sin fell away. My tears and the perfume mingled together and I wiped His feet with my hair.

There was uproar! But not from Him, He smiled and gently helped me to my feet.

Someone complained that the perfume was expensive  and could have been saved for the poor.  He told them that there would always be poor people, but that they would not always have Him.

Someone else was quick to point out my reputation, after all I was a sinful woman, but He told them I had done a beautiful thing in preparing Him for burial  - that had not been my intention but I was pleased He liked what I had done.

The dinner host and his guests condemned me.

Jesus forgave me.

And I washed His feet with my perfume and my tears and dried them with my hair.

## Pause for thought:

- What does being forgiven mean for us?

- If we are forgiven can we forgive others, and what might that look like for us?

## A widow's offering
## The voice of Andrew

We were there in the temple with Him again, the way we had been many times before. We were all there, the twelve of us and some of the women who had followed Him from the beginning.

We had gone to pray, but as we had come to expect, nothing was ever straightforward with Him. Many people grouped together, a few women congregated in the courtyard and several men entered the main part of the temple almost as one. We hovered in the doorway waiting for instruction, teaching or blessing. We had not yet grasped that the blessing would come from Him.

He ushered us through the gates, and deep into the heart of the temple and there He began to teach us.

"Look," He said, "Watch as the men of wealth give their offerings to God. They give little of what they have and keep much for themselves. They give little, not only from their pockets but also from their very souls," He told us.

He paused, for breath and for effect. He wanted us to take it all in, but I'm not sure we did, I'm not sure we really understood.

"Look," He continued "Watch as the widow places her last two coins into the plate - this is all that she has and yet she gives it willingly to her God. She offers all that she can, the little money she possesses and all of herself."

We did as we were told, we looked.

We looked and we saw the men of wealth giving little and we looked and saw the bent over old widow giving all she had, but what were we to do next?

Did He want us to go to her and lend her money or did he want us to rebuke the men for not giving enough? We did not know or understand what He wanted from us.

Years later we recalled the scene and reflected on what Jesus was trying to tell us. It is important that whatever we have we give generously back to God so that he can use it to further the kingdom.

Pause for thought:

- Let us reflect for ourselves, are we like the wealthy men who gave a little of a lot, or are we like the widow who gave everything she had to God's glory?

# Maundy

# Thursday

## A dusty room
## The voice of Larry, the house owner

They came unexpectedly. Two of them following a man with a jar - he pointed me out, and then disappeared as the others hurried towards me. I recognised them immediately; they were followers of Him, the teacher.

We had spoken before, this teacher and I, He spoke wisely and seemed somehow to be able to look inside my very soul.

We had discussed money, something that I was very fond of, but He seemed to think that I should give more away, help the local poor, reach out to those in need around me. I was a little taken aback; after all, who was this man to tell me what I should do with my own money?

But He sowed a seed, and it really got me thinking. It was as if He knew it would, as if He even knew the outcome of my thinking.

Then of course it happened, his two disciples arrived and asked for my upper room so that they and the teacher could share the Passover together.

Here was my chance, to show Him that I had been thinking about our conversation. I welcomed the party and told them I would prepare it for them.

They went back to give Jesus the news and I went straight to the room that had not been used for a while and needed a good clean. I spent the afternoon cleaning everywhere, making it ready to receive Him.

It was not too long before they showed up. Everyone looked hot and bothered, He smiled at me as I had said nothing about charging Him for the use of the room. He knew I was beginning to change.

He asked me for a bowl of water, which I provided and then to everyone's amazement He bent down and washed his disciples' feet. I have never seen a teacher, a leader do that before. Who was this man who turned the norm on its head and changed everything from the inside out?

<u>Pause for thought:</u>

- Jesus encourages Larry to give up some of his money to the poor, what might Jesus be asking us to give away?

- How might we have felt if Jesus knelt and washed our feet?

## Uncork the bottle
## The voice of Ruth, a servant girl

I was there that night. I was doing my job – setting the table, clearing up the leftovers and corking the bottles of wine.

My name is Ruth and I am a servant girl, owned by the man who let that upper room. I was told to get there early, prepare the room, clean up, uncork the wine and stay out of sight. I did what I was told, but I didn't stay out of sight. I couldn't, He wouldn't let me.

They arrived, twelve of them and Him. They were tired, hungry and thirsty, and wanting to celebrate together. They didn't see me, but He did, He even called me by my name.

He asked me for a bowl of water and a towel and of course I obliged, but I didn't know why. Everything was clean, I had done it myself. But soon it all became very clear. He knelt at the feet of His friends and washed them. One was quite upset, but he calmed down when Jesus spoke with him.

And then stranger than strange, He called me over to the table. He asked for more bread and another bottle of wine to be uncorked, and I did my bit.

He told me to stay and share, much to the others' discomfort, but it was His party and He wanted me to be present. He took the bread in His hands. It was mesmerizing. He gave thanks to God and He broke it.

But this was not the end; He shared it among us and told us that from here on in, every time we ate bread together we should remember Him. He spoke of His body broken, but I did not know what He meant, neither did anyone else I am sure.

Next He took the wine that I had uncorked for Him and poured it into a cup, again He gave thanks to God and shared it out among us. When you drink it, He said, remember the new promise I make between you and God. We all thought that maybe He had had a little too much wine.

He spoke to one of His friends, telling him that he would betray Him, and to another, saying that he would deny Him. They were all adamant that they would stick with Him whatever happened next. Little did anyone know, apart from Him, what would really happen next.

They left the upper room singing; I remained, and cleaned up. Later I heard the story of the events in the garden, a bogus trial, and the death of the man for whom I had uncorked the wine, the man who had called me by name and a man who by His love in action showed me God.

Pause for thought:

- How might you have felt if you have been in Ruth's position?

- How might you have reacted to Jesus washing the feet of his friends?

## He offered me bread and wine
## The voice of Judas

He offered me bread and told me to eat, and He offered me the cup of wine and told me to drink. Even though He knew that it was I who would betray him.

I could tell He knew it was me, just by the way His eyes met mine when He asked us the question, and as He held me fixed in His gaze. As the others bickered among themselves, He knew.

And it had all begun so differently. What had brought us here? To share this bread and this wine in this upper room, while clubs and spears lay dormant?

It had all seemed so easy then, three years ago. He had gathered a team around Him, a mini army. We would be the catalyst for the nation to grow, and fight and be free. We would send the Romans packing, reclaim our land and taste freedom.

And He, I believed, He was the man to do it. He spoke of a new kingdom of justice and peace where equality ruled and no-one was enslaved.

But He is so slow. The momentum had faded and almost gone, but our priests were getting increasingly angered by Him. And we, his followers, were getting increasingly sucked in. I was ready to make a stand, to speak out, to get the ball rolling, I was willing to light the fire.

And the authorities knew me only too well. They too were getting impatient, they wanted rid of Him, He was making far too many waves.

They offered me money, you see, money that could be used to buy new weapons, or perhaps feed the poor. So I took it.

And soon, when the right time comes, I will slip away and tell them where they can find him.

I will hand him over for thirty pieces of silver. This man who offers me bread and wine; who looks deep into my soul; who somehow knows what I will do.

But He does not rebuke me, or try to talk me out of it, or even pick me up on it. It is almost as if He is urging me on, willing me to do it, in order to fulfil some kind of greater plan.

Maybe there's an army just waiting for its cue, to rise up and attack and this is all a part of the plot. So I am doing my part to usher in a new kingdom. Well, we will see, we will see.


Pause for thought:

- Judas plots to betray Jesus; have we willingly or unwillingly betrayed anyone?

- What might that feel like?

- How do we think Jesus might have felt?

## And I couldn't watch one hour
## The voice of James

We followed Him from the upper room where we had celebrated the Passover together. We followed Him into the garden, as we had followed Him so many times before. But something had changed this time; I couldn't put my finger on it then, but there was a definite change.

Maybe it had been when He knelt and washed our feet, or the words He said when offering us bread and wine, or the sadness in His eyes, or the unrest in His spirit, or maybe it was a combination of all of the above. We would change too, but we didn't understand that either.

The garden was still, quiet and peaceful, to begin with. It was pleasant to soak up the atmosphere, we had eaten well, and wine had flowed; it was late and we were tired, ready for a well earned, and much needed sleep. But Jesus' distress was clear.

He took Peter, John and I deeper into the wooded part of the garden, leaving the others where they were. We could feel the tension in the air, could almost cut it, but we didn't really understand. He asked us to stay awake, keep watch, and pray with Him, that was all He asked. And I couldn't watch but one hour.

He walked away, silence fell, tiredness crept over me, prayer dwindled, eyes grew heavy, and sleep came. I couldn't watch but one hour with him, and that is all He had asked of me.

He returned, more broken than when He had left, more sad and unsure, and found me asleep. What kind of a disciple was I that I couldn't watch but one hour with Him? He shook me, woke me, rebuked me, and allowed me to try again as He went back to his praying.

And again sleep came all too easily. My heart longed to stay awake, to watch and pray with Him, but I was weak. Maybe if I had known what was going to happen next, maybe then I could have watched, waited, hoped, helped, who knows?

Suddenly, the peace of the garden was shattered. Men with clubs, lanterns and swords rushed towards us. I was awake then, bewildered, but alert and terrified. What did they want, these men that came in the dead of night, could it really be as He had said it would be?

And then, a betrayer's kiss, a moment of defiance, a solider in pain, a healing, an arrest, ropes that bound, fear that struck, the escorts' departure, His friends fleeing and then silence.

And I could not watch but one hour, what kind of friend does that make me?

### Pause for thought:

- James was asked to stay awake, to watch and pray but one hour; can we this Maundy Thursday, or anytime, watch and pray with Christ?

- Reflect on the times when we may have let Jesus down.

## And I warmed myself by the fire
## The voice of Peter

He told me I would do it, deny Him I mean. And I was so sure that He was wrong. I even argued with Him, thought I knew best, believed I was strong, that I would go all the way, to death if I had to, with Him and for Him.

How wrong I was.

After his arrest, everyone scattered, fear overtook us. We didn't want to be next. I wanted to run and hide as well, but something compelled me to follow the mob, to see where they took Him, where He would end up. I followed at a distance, not so close as to get myself arrested but close enough so as not to lose sight of them.

They entered the courtyard to the governor's palace. They disappeared inside and I warmed myself by the fire and tried to blend in.

It wasn't long before they questioned me. Are you not a Galilean? Are you not one of them? Are you not with Him?

The choice was mine, I could have stood up to be counted as His, could have called Him friend, told them what He meant to me, what He meant to so many.

But I didn't.

I was frightened, not that that's an excuse but... but I wasn't really ready to die back then, wasn't willing to put my life on the line for Him, as He had done for me, but I didn't understand that either. It was all a bit of a fog.

Three times I denied Him, just as He said I would. Three times I said I didn't even know Him, let alone called Him friend, teacher, master, or Lord.

And there I was, warming myself by the fire, trying to blend in, when just as He said it would, the cock crowed.

Suddenly, I knew what I had done. The enormity of it all hit me between the eyes. Judas had betrayed Him, His friends had deserted Him, and I... I, the one He had called the rock, the one who had called Him Messiah, I had denied Him.

I fell to the ground, put my head in my hands and wept.

Jesus had stood alone before Pilate, and what did I do? I warmed myself by the fire and tried to blend in.

<u>Pause for thought:</u>

- Peter had a choice - to stand and be counted for Christ or not. If we are faced with a similar choice, what would we do?

- Reflect on times when we may have denied our faith in Christ.

## I was sure he was one of them
## The voice of Rachel, a servant

I was sure he was one of them as he stood and warmed himself by the fire. At first I said nothing, I did not want to cause any trouble and he looked like all he wanted to do was blend in. I kept myself to myself as I always did; I had learnt the hard way about speaking out of turn.

But then someone else approached him, and asked if he had come with the one they called Jesus, the one that was under guard in the high priest's palace.

"No," he answered, "Not me, I am not with Him." Then I knew for sure that he was indeed one of them. He spoke with a Galilean accent, it was unmistakable.

I tried to convince myself that I wanted to stay out of it, but really I wanted to know more about this man Jesus, I wanted his friend and follower to give me the inside story, I wanted to know what all the fuss was about.

Was He really the King of the Jews who had come to set His people free? To set me free. Was He really the man that would or could change the world, and how would He do it now if He was bound and on trial before the authorities? How could He change things now?

The questions in my head overpowered me; rational thinking had gone out of the window. "You are one of them, I'm sure," I blurted out. Everyone turned and stared straight at me before turning their accusing gazes on him.

"No," he said, "No I'm not," as a heavy silence descended around the fire.

Later another visitor in town asked again, I had stayed around just in case he changed his mind and divulged all about the king from Nazareth.

But a third time the Galilean denied he even knew Him. Scared, I presumed, of what it would mean if he admitted he knew this Jesus, worried for his own skin, but I guess I don't blame him.

A cock crowed, and the man at the fire ran away, hiding his head in his hands and crying like a baby. Reality had hit home with a crash, three times he had denied His lord, master and friend, just as he had been told he would.

Pause for thought:

- Rachel wanted to know more about Jesus from His friend; will we be willing to tell others about our friend Jesus?

- Reflect on missed opportunities to share the gospel of Christ.

# Good Friday

# It should have been me
## The voice of Barabbas

I sat, chained and feeling sorry for myself. I knew that prison would hold me until death approached, and I knew that would not be long.

I sat trying to focus my mind on other things, but the slamming of prison doors and the jangle of keys made the task impossible. I soon found myself imagining execution, the crowd, the humiliation, the pain and eventually death.

I was in a dark place, but I had put myself there, I only had myself to blame. It was just desserts for the pain and suffering I had caused others, not that I would have admitted that to anyone else, of course.

But in the darkness I thought I heard my name being called. Maybe it had been my imagination, or maybe it was the voices of hell calling for me, but no, to my surprise it was the crowd. They were shouting my name, not in anger, not screaming for my blood, but in triumph, appealing for my freedom.

But why?

What strange turn of events had masterminded this, how was it that I could walk away from this a free man?

The guards arrived, unchained me and led me out into the light and the awaiting crowd. But on the way I passed Him.

He was locked in the cell next to mine, badly beaten, bruised and broken, but His eyes haunted me, they always will.

It was the Passover. I knew the Governor had a custom to release a prisoner at that time, but I had never believed it would be me.

But why was it me?

Here was a man who stood for justice and fair play, I was a man who fought for what I wanted, and took out anyone who stood in my way. Here was a man who preached love and peace and all I knew was hatred and war. Who was this man that stood in my place, who took the death that was due to me?

Who was He? They called Him Jesus and because of Him I am free.

Pause for thought:

- What does freedom mean for us?

- What does it mean that Jesus has taken the punishment for us?

## I hardly dared to breathe
## The voice of Pilate's servant

I hardly dared take a breath as I continued about my work around the house, minding my own business, keeping my head down. I knew that things had been strained in the household, I had felt it.

I worked for the wife of the Governor, Pontius Pilate. I had been in post for many years when it happened and the mistress had shared many things with me. And that night, I remember, she shared her dreams and fears with me, as I share them with you now.

It was a few nights before that that the nightmares began - the same one every night. She would wake up in a sweat and could hardly draw breath; her dreams were turning her into a nervous wreck.

The dreams were of Him, this Jesus character that had transformed the whole of Jerusalem, Jews and Romans alike. Some had changed for the better, some for the worse. And now my mistress's dreams saw Him bound and beaten standing in front of her husband, who was to pass judgement on Him.

The man had eyes that bore into her very soul, she said. He was not angry, or full of hatred, in fact He stared at her and her husband with compassion and even love, not that she was very good at recognising that emotion.

The dream had warned her to stay away from this man, to leave him to the Jews, to do with him as they willed, but Pilate just had to get involved. He said that he had no choice, that the crowd were threatening him with going to Rome, to the Emperor. It could have meant losing everything.

The position, the power, and all that comes with that, the honour, the glory, the praise of Rome.  But instead they lost even more than that, they lost their very selves.

Jesus came, just as the dream predicted, Pilate got involved, again as predicted.  He tried to walk away, to wash his hands of the whole sordid affair, but it was too late by then, the die had already been cast.

Jesus was led away, stripped, whipped, and crucified, and for Pilate and my mistress, the real nightmare began.

Pause for thought:

- Pilate's servant was required to be a loyal friend. Reflect on a time when we are needed to walk alongside someone in a difficult situation.

## And I tried to tell him
## The voice of Pilate's wife

And I tried to tell him, to tell him not to get involved, to walk away, to wash his hands, but he never listened to me, and now he is paying the price - we all are.

I tried to tell him that I had a dream, that I saw the man, standing battered and bruised in our house, chained and beaten, broken and alone, and yet there was something different about him. He did not curse, or hate, He was somehow open and calling me to him. Not for me to help Him, but so that somehow He could help me. I didn't really understand, but I knew He was special, His eyes full of love told me that.

And I tried to tell my husband, I told him not to get involved, to pass him over, and to let the Jews do their own dirty work. They had never wanted his help before, so why now did they come seeking his approval? Because they wanted this man dead, that's why, and only Roman law could do that, and Pilate had the final say.

They played on his insecurities, questioning his loyalty to Caesar, trying to make out that Jesus was after Caesar's job, putting Pilate's on the line as well, and he liked his job... usually.

I tried to tell him not to get involved, so after sending Jesus to Herod, and having him flogged, and offering the people a choice of who they wanted to save, he washed his hands. He let his soldiers take Him, mock Him, nail Him to a tree and we watched Him die.

I tried to tell him not to get involved, but it was too late, and now Jesus' blood is on his hands.

Now he washes, and daydreams, and he wonders how it might have been if he had listened to me, if he had walked away, if he had not got involved with the man from Galilee.

Who was this man who stirred up such violent anger, and who brought grown men to their knees? And who now, even in death, haunts us all?

I tried to tell him not to get involved, but he never listened to me.

Pause for thought:

- Are there times and situations where it is right for us not to get involved?

- If so, what might they be?

# And it was just another lash of the whip
## The voice of Marcus – a soldier

And it was just another lash of the whip, leather strips entwined with bone, gathered together to form a handle and placed into my hand.

And it was just another lash of the whip, just another order followed; another criminal sentenced and another punishment administered.

And it was just another lash of the whip; another back ripped open, more flesh torn and yet more blood spilled.

And we had done it so many times before, to extract a confession, an admission of guilt. Trying to get a prisoner to see it our way, the Roman way, the only way.

And it was just another lash of the whip, another soul broken, and another spirit crushed.

But not with Him. He was different. He was tried, but not humbled. He was beaten, but not broken. He was in agony but He did not curse, or abuse, or hate, or even say a word. There was only the odd grunt of pain and the sharp, violent, involuntary intake of breath.

That was all.

And it was just another lash of the whip, a roar of the crowd, a shout for his blood, and a score settled.

And yet , I will never forget the way He looked at me. The way His eyes were full of love for one who hated so much.

So, who was that man, and what were we doing but following orders?

How can we, I, be held to account?

And the questions rage, the rumours fly and something inside me begins to ache, like it has never done before.

And it was just another lash of the whip.

But it wasn't.

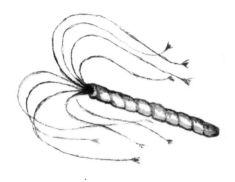

### Pause for thought:

- Marcus claimed he was only following orders. How do we react to that?

- Have there been times in our lives when we have followed orders before our Christian faith?

## But he deserved it
## The voice of Mark - a thief

I remember the day as if it were yesterday. He was my friend, my colleague if you like, my brother in arms, my partner in crime, but that day changed my life forever.

My name is Mark. I am a former criminal, a foe of the nation, an enemy of the state, once, but now things are different and all because of that one day and that one man - that man Jesus.

It was my friend who hung on that cross next to Him, my friend who took his just punishment, my friend who asked for forgiveness and my friend who was offered paradise with Him. Let me tell you about it.

We made a living from stealing. We took what was not ours, just to get ahead, just because we felt the world owed us something. We told everyone that would listen that we knew no better, but we did.

We played the game, and we were caught. He, Barney, my friend, was arrested. I ran. I was only out to save my own skin, I left him high and dry. My friend was tried for the crime we had both committed. He was sentenced to death and I was free.

The day of execution came; I stood, ashamed, in the background and watched. It was not hard to blend in as there were thousands of people lining the streets that day.

Yet they did not seek the demise of my friend, but the end of Him. The one they called the Messiah, the King of the Jews, Jesus of Nazareth.

He too had been tried, in a mock court, and sentenced to an unjust death, and with my friend he was led to the Place of the Skull and crucified there. A third was strung up that day, who mocked the Christ and hurled insults at him. But my friend had seen in Jesus what many others had missed. He had seen the light of God shining in His face and knew that He was indeed who He claimed to be.

My friend accepted the punishment for his crime and asked this Jesus to help him start again.

"Jesus, remember me when you come into your kingdom," I heard him utter.

He was rewarded. "Truly I tell you, today you will be with me in paradise," Jesus said.

So now I journey on, without my friend and partner in crime, but now I am a changed man. I no longer believe that the world owes me, and I am now looking for ways in which I can give back.

And all because of that one day and that one offer of paradise, not only for my friend but for me and for all.

### Pause for thought:

- What do we think an offer of paradise might mean to us?

- Reflect on times when we may have felt guilty and in need of forgiveness and a chance to start again.

## You would have done the same
## The voice of Titus the Priest

Believe me, if it had been you, you would have done the same.

This man Jesus was threatening our livelihood, our very existence. He was trying to turn our whole system of belief on its head by talking about knowing God personally.

How can you ever know the Almighty personally? I mean, what rot. God is God, never to be spoken of in human terms.

And then He went even further, claiming He was God's chosen one, God's only Son – maybe even divine. What else could we do? We couldn't have Him going around saying things like that, could we?

If it had been you, you would have done the same.

He called us a brood of vipers, and said that we were only out for ourselves. He made out that we moved in some sort of inner circle, and He told stories, stories that painted us as cold and heartless human beings.

But we have families too; we have wives and children that depend on us. If we were made unclean by helping a beaten and bruised Samaritan, we would have missed our turn in the temple and that means no hours, no pay and no food for the table.

Now tell me that you would not have done the same.

He talked of destroying the temple in three days, the temple that His forefathers had sweated blood and tears to build. He spoke of the synagogue being within us and that God was accessible to all, not just the Jews. Not just God for God's chosen people, but for all people. But how could that really be the case?

The man was a nightmare; if it had been you, you would have done the same.

We only thought what everyone else was thinking. Get rid of the man, stop Him from whipping up the crowd into a frenzy, and keep Him from trespassing on God's laws and sacred places.

He was in the wrong, not us. He was the one who alleged He could forgive sins. How dare He, only God could do that. He was the one who touched the unclean, dined with sinners and made friends with Roman tax collectors. He was the one who rode into the city on a donkey acting like He was some kind of king, and allowing the people to fall at his feet. The same people who so easily came to see things our way only a few days later. He was the one who brought it all on himself. We were not to blame.

It was His doing, He was the maker of His own downfall, and I know if it had been you, you would have done the same.


## Pause for thought:

- Can you identify with the priests' way of thinking?

## A second mother
## The voice of John, the beloved disciple

Everything changed that day – no, that's not quite true. Everything changed the first day He came into our lives. The day He called us to leave all that we knew and loved and follow Him. We were all so unsure initially, but there was something about Him, something compelling and worth fighting for.

However, it wasn't long before we were glad to follow Him; we knew that He was unique, that He had more to give than anyone before or since. He had the gift of life to give, and He gave it freely.

We followed as He moved from place to place, teaching, healing, and offering a chance to all, regardless of race, creed or colour, to meet and walk with the living God.

Thousands journeyed with us – wanting Him to touch them, bless them and change them and He did. Hopes ran high; many believed that He would raise an army and fight to set people free from the tyranny of Rome. Yet there were no clubs, no spears, no talk of hatred at all, only compassion and love.

In spite of that, there were people who hated him; they were wary of his talk of God, and the relationship He claimed to have with the Almighty. They arrested Him, we were there that night and we ran and hid. They tried him, in a manner of speaking, and they sentenced him to death on a cross.

I was there that day, standing at the foot of His cross, cradling his mother in my arms, as her pain was so hard to bear.

I was there, as He looked down at us, somehow smiling through His agony, and He spoke to his mother in hers.

"Woman, behold your son." That's what he said. He wanted me to be that son; He wanted me somehow to take His place, but I did not know how.

Then He turned His head to me. "Here is your mother," He said, and then I began to understand, I knew what I had to do. I held her tight, and wiped her tears from her eyes. I would look after her from here on in.

Now I would love her the way He loved her, the way He loved all of us. I took her home, just like He told me to; life would never be the same. But why would I want it to be? Through his death, life and hope live on.

## Pause for thought:

- Think of a time when God has asked you to do a seemingly impossible task.

- How did you respond?

# Another roll of the dice
## The voice of Marco – a Roman soldier.

And it was just another roll of the dice, or so I thought. Just another game. Another criminal, another crucifixion, another job and another day at the office.

But I was wrong. This was unusual; this was more about life than death. He was distinctive, the way He looked at me, not with hatred in his eyes as I had come to expect, but with love and forgiveness.

I was on execution duty that day, not my favourite part of the job, but we all have to take our turn. The prisoners had been placed into our hands at the city gate and it was our job to escort them to the Place of the Skull and crucify them there. There were three that day, two others and Him.

Who was he? This man from Galilee, who had succeeded in bringing the wrath of the whole Jewish nation upon himself and the rage of all of Rome.

Who was He? This man, who when the crowd shouted crucify, uttered "Father, forgive." Who was He? This man, that when we drove nails into His hands and feet, said we didn't know what we were doing.

We lifted him skyward upon that wooden cross. It was our job, we were under orders. How could we do anything else? We had bills to pay, families to feed, and quotas to meet.

And it was just another roll of the dice. The crowd shouted, the priests mocked, several women wept, and we played dice. Rolling for His coat, a part of Him, not because of who He was, but because it was a nice coat.

He cried out that He was thirsty; so I took a sponge, soaked it in vinegar, put it on a stick and lifted it to His mouth. His broken eyes met mine. I was transfixed; it was if He almost smiled at me.

Suddenly, it was not just another roll of the dice, another game, it was real.

And as He bowed His head and died, I found life.

Who was this man, who changed our game into reality, who rolled a different dice, and through His death, gave me life?

Truly this man is the Son of God.

## Pause for thought:

- Have you ever thought of life as a game?

- If you have, is there anything or anyone for which you would risk everything?

## A mother's cry
## The voice of Mary

I listened, but only because I had no choice.

I heard, but only because I needed to.

I watched, but only because He was my son, and I winced and I crumbled inside, because of what they did to Him.

He was and is my son, He always will be. I held Him, cared for Him, and comforted Him when He cried.

Now, I could do nothing. Now I felt helpless and useless. I hid my eyes, but I could not hide my tears, as they flogged Him, mocked Him, and drove Him out of the city with a cross upon His back.

I followed, close enough, but not too close, in love and pain. As I did so, I began to remember his birth, the presents from the strangers, and the man in the temple. He told me my heart would break, and now it was breaking, with every step He took to His death.

I looked on in horror as they pushed Him to the ground, stripped Him of his clothes, and nailed Him to the wooden cross.

I could hardly breathe as they lifted it skyward, and jerked it into place.

I felt His pain, almost as if it were my own, and in some strange way it was.

The crowd was full of anger; they who only days before had hailed Him as their king now laughed and ridiculed Him.

The priests ordered Him to save himself. The Romans rolled dice for His clothes, and His friends - they had deserted Him long before.

Only I stood watching, near enough to hear Him cry:
"Father forgive them, they do not know what they are doing."

I saw and felt His agony. The nails in His hands and feet, the crown of thorns upon his head, but more that that, the moment of separation from His Father's side.

I watched the sky turn black, and heard the temple curtain rip, as He uttered: "It is finished!"

I cried every tear I had left to cry, a mother's heart broken in two, and the hope of the nation dashed. They dragged me away; nothing left to see, just my son's broken body, hanging on the tree.

Pause for thought:

- Could you put yourself in Mary's shoes?

- How might you feel if it were your child?

# The curtain was torn

Listen to the roar of the crowd, the mocking laughter, the crack of the whip on His back.

Look into the faces of the priests and scribes, that speak of victory; see the eagerness of the Roman soldiers as they gamble for what little He has, and gaze upon the tear stained faces of those that love Him.

Smell the fear - the fear of those hanging beside Him, and the stench of the blood left on instruments of torture which are now thrown haphazardly on the ground.

Look around - where do you stand? Are you there at the foot of His cross, or hiding somewhere behind?

Listen to Him crying out to His Father, "My God, my God, why have you forsaken me?" And hear the mocking voices that only days before had hailed Him as king.

Watch, as darkness covers the earth, as the very foundations on which you stand shake, as rocks split apart and the tombs of the righteous are wrenched open.

Strain your ears and dimly heed the curtain in the temple as it is torn from top to bottom, and try to understand what difference that will make to your very existence.

This is because, for as long as you and the people before you have known, the Holy of Holies in the temple, has been a no-go zone.

It was only accessed if you happened to be the High Priest that year. The curtain separated the Ark of the Covenant, the place of God, from the people of God. But now, on this day and with His death, the curtain is torn apart and God is, therefore, accessible to all.

Look around - where do you stand? Are you there at the foot of His cross, or hiding somewhere behind?

Examine the scene, as you and everyone around you wonders who this man really is. This man, who is dying in front of your very eyes, and yet the question of his true identity rages on.

For some, He is a convicted criminal getting His just desserts. For some, He is the man who they thought would rally an army, and fight with chariot and war horse against the Romans for freedom and peace. For others, He is a friend, dying an agonising death upon a cross, and for the few, for those who have seen beyond death to a new life, He is the Christ, the Son of God, the promised one, the Messiah.

Look around - where do you stand? Are you there at the foot of His cross, or hiding somewhere behind?

Move closer to the cross, hear Him utter those final words, "It is finished!" and observe, as He bows His head and dies.

Look around - where do you stand? Are you there at the foot of His cross, or hiding somewhere behind?

### Pause for thought:

- What does it mean for you, that the curtain was torn and access to God was opened up?

# It wasn't me!

It wasn't me who betrayed Him, surely that was Judas, with his hands firmly in the till, without a care for anyone but himself.

It wasn't me who denied Him, surely that was Peter, so worried that he too may end up dead.

It wasn't me who shouted "Crucify" - surely that was the crowd, with fickle minds, who are far too easily led.

It wasn't me who washed my hands, surely that was Pilate, too afraid to stand up, and upset the authorities.

It wasn't me who flogged Him, or drove the nails home, surely that was the soldiers, under orders, unable to disobey.

It wasn't me that mocked and jeered, surely that was the priests, concerned about their own identity, and their own lives.

And it wasn't me who left Him dying alone, surely that was His friends, who ran in fear.

However, today on this Good Friday, over 2000 years on, I look and see that Jesus is crucified again. And as I look more closely, I see the part I play, hear the words "Forgive them," and know that they are for me.

It is me who betrays Him, each time I turn away, and hurt a fellow human with the things I do or say.

It is me who denies Him, each time I do not stand and fight against injustice, or lend a helping hand.

It is me who shouts out "Crucify", for I'm of fickle mind; it's easier to run with the crowd, and leave the cross behind.

It is me who washes my hands, and in doing so, I wash away the guilt. I refuse to see this Jesus, and the New World He has built.

It is me who flogs and nails him upon the wooden tree, but how quick I am to forget that He died to set me free.

It is me who mocks and jeers, as if I didn't care, but after all He's done for me, what makes me think I dare?

It is me who leaves Him dying, out in the cold and rain. I begin to see more clearly now that I have caused His pain.

So Jesus is my Saviour, who I see now that I've killed, but with resurrection glory, my life will soon be filled.


### Pause for thought:

- Can you identify aspects of yourself in this meditation?

- Have there ever been times when you have done or experienced similar things?

# Easter Sunday

## It was the last thing I could do for Him
## The voice of Mary Magdalene

I didn't know what to do!!!
I didn't know which way to turn.
My world had been completely twisted upside down and inside out.
And it was not my world.
Everyone was affected and changed.
Everyone that was there, everyone that heard, and everyone that engaged: second and third hand after that.
It was the weekend that changed the world forever.
Let me tell you about it.

It was dark and cold, my eyes were sore from crying and grief was the only emotion I understood. The weekend had been blacker than black and every flicker of hope had been destroyed.

We had held Him in such esteem, we had believed that He was the one. We had walked with Him, listened to Him, heard His stories and witnessed the miracles. We had caught a glimpse of the New Jerusalem that He had told us about, but then it was all gone.

He was arrested, and tried in some mock court.
Beaten, and ridiculed and led out to die a criminal's death.

He was alone, betrayed, denied and deserted by his friends. Only the women folk looked on, unable to speak out, unable to stand.

Then came the Sabbath - nothing could be done then.
But the morning came, and, as it was the last thing I could do for Him, I gladly did it. I gathered herbs and spices and some of the other women and while it was still dark we journeyed to His tomb to anoint His body.

We didn't think ahead: what would we say to the guards on duty? How would we move the stone away? We would cross that bridge when we came to it, we thought.

But when we got there;
There was no bridge to cross, there were no guards, no stone, nothing. There was not even a body. Just some folded grave clothes and a shining light.

"He's not here - He has risen," we were told.
But what did that mean?

We ran to get Peter and the others to explain that someone had stolen the body of our Lord.

Two came running, Peter and John to see that everything was just as we had said. They went away dismayed, but I lingered; I could not tear myself away.

Suddenly a memory stirred in my mind.
A light of revelation sparked.

A gardener stood by, a gardener that called me by name, And then my vision cleared, I understood, I was speaking with my Lord.

I fell at His feet and clung to Him. He was alive – just as He had said He would be and I didn't want to lose Him again.

"Don't stay, don't cling, go and tell!" He told me.
He sent me out. What was I to do? Stay silent or stand up, speak out and change the world around me, as He had changed mine?

It was the last thing I could do for Him!!!

<u>Pause for thought:</u>

- Have you heard Jesus calling you by name?

- What does that look like for you?

- Has Christ changed your life?

- What have you done or what do you intend to do about it?

- Will you stay silent or stand up and shout about how Christ has changed your life?

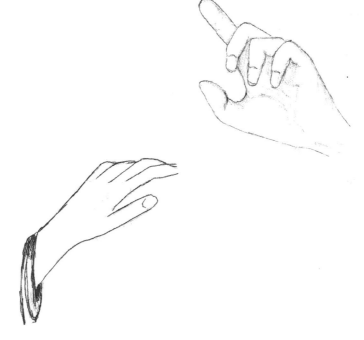

## I gave him my tomb
## The voice of Joseph of Arimathea

I couldn't understand it when I heard the news.
It had been my tomb, you see.
I had been the one to ask Pilate for Jesus' body before the Sabbath began.
I had been someone whose heart had been changed by Him.

I had been one of them, you see. A priest in the temple.
I had heard of their plots to arrest him. I knew of the dodgy trial that was planned and of the witnesses that had been handsomely paid to tell lies. I knew that they had bought off Judas, and that money in his hands was always going to be worth more than his loyalty. I stood and watched from a  distance, and did nothing to intervene.

I knew of the vicious streak that ran through them.
Each and every one of them.  I knew because it was the same ruthless streak that had once run through me.

That was until I met Him.  Here was a man that knew the scriptures far better than I did.

A man that understood God, more deeply than I ever could.
A man who spoke of a kingdom built on love and not on rules.  A man who put others before Himself, even to the point of death.

So, I did what little I could.

I asked for His body and buried Him in my own tomb.

But now his friends have told me that my tomb could not Hold him, that death has been defeated and that He lives.

I do not know how this can be.
But I want to know more,
I want to believe,
I want to be changed,
And I want to be counted for Him.

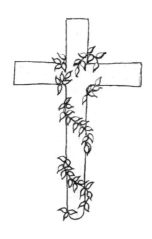

Pause for thought:

- What might we give to Jesus in the way that Joseph gave his tomb?

- How might we show that our hearts have been changed?

## And how our hearts burned within us!!!
## The voice of Cleopas' wife

And how our hearts burned within us
as we turned and ran back towards Jerusalem.
Somehow we had been given new life and we wanted to make the most of
it and share it with everyone.

Hold on - before we get ahead of ourselves let's start from the beginning.

It had been a week full of high emotions.
You see, our friend and master, dare I say, Lord,
had been taken from us.

At the start He had rode triumphantly into the city, the people had loved
Him, they even hailed Him as their king.
But hearts, minds and loyalties are soon swayed.
A few words from a priest or two, a threatening look from a Roman
soldier and the same crowd is shouting "Crucify."

Jesus was arrested, tried, put to death and buried even before the Sabbath
began.

There was nothing left for us in Jerusalem, so while it was still dark, we
began our journey home.

We were down, my husband Cleopas and I, we had hit rock bottom.
We didn't know what to do with ourselves.

Even His stories, that had once seemed unforgettable, were now
beginning to fade in our memories.

At first we walked alone, in silence, but later we were joined by a man. A man who noticed our tear-stained faces and questioned us. He appeared to have no idea what had happened. How you could have been in Jerusalem and have missed it was beyond me. But he wanted to know, so we told him. He listened intently, and when we had finished he spoke, and as he did he explained the Holy Scriptures to us. We were amazed.

Finally we reached our destination.
He went to leave us, but we invited him in.
We sat, to share a meal.
He said the blessing and broke bread.

Suddenly his identity was clear.
Here was Jesus,
Our Lord and master, alive and present with us.

He disappeared, and we drew new breath.
We knew that we had just encountered the risen Christ. We could hardly believe it, but still half dazed we headed back to the city.

Our hopes renewed. Our spirits soaring and our hearts burning within us.

Ready and willing to testify that Jesus Christ was alive.


## Pause for thought:

- Has there ever been a time when our hearts have burned within us?

- If so what did we do about it?

# I should have believed
## The voice of Thomas

I was not there at the beginning, well, I was, but I was not there at the beginning of the end. Stop. What do I mean? Let me explain.

I was there at the beginning, when He first called me, and asked me to follow him. I was there, when we moved from place to place and I watched Him teach, heal and show us God.

I was there when they arrested Him, tried Him, crucified Him and buried Him. But when He rose again, and stood among His friends in that upper room, I was not there.

I was grieving, feeling sorry for myself, I needed to be alone, to nurse my open wounds, and to start looking to rebuild my shattered life. Not that that is any kind of an excuse of course, but it is the reason why I wasn't there.

But Jesus, being Jesus, did not leave it there, even when I refused to believe the stories I was told. I doubted, and I needed proof. I wanted to touch His hands where the nails had left their mark and place my hand where the spear had pierced his side. I sought the truth, it was vital I was sure, before I just took the word of the others, who had loved him as much as I did.

What a fool I was!

Of course He came again, and this time I was there, He made sure of that. And He gave me the proof I so longed for. I touched the signs of crucifixion, I felt my shame inside me like a knife, forever doubting him, and I fell at His feet and called Him Lord.

He never condemned me, or rebuked me, He just smiled, happy that I now believed. But He challenged me. "You believed because you have seen me, happy are those that believe without seeing me," He said.

What did he mean?

As the days and weeks passed, it all began to be clear. I should have remembered all the things He had told us. I should have trusted my friends, I should have believed that I stood in the presence of God and man, but I didn't.

So, where did we go from there?

As I said, I was there, from the beginning to the end, and back to the beginning again. Nothing was ever the same.

How could it be?

With Jesus risen, ascended to His father, and the Holy Spirit living and breathing among us. And we, humble fishermen, turned into prophets and teachers almost overnight. We were now His hands and feet, we were to be Christ to the world.

## Pause for thought:

- How do we feel about the challenge that is set down for us to be Christ's hands and feet to the world?

- How might we begin to be them for people today?

# Epilogue

If you intend to use this book to journey with Jesus through Lent and Holy Week, here are a few Bible readings and prayers to use individually or collectively that may assist your reflections.

(All biblical quotations have been taken from the New Revised Standard Version)

## Jesus  -  name above all names

Jesus,
Promised Messiah
Born in a stable
But born to be King.

Jesus,
King of Kings
Worshipped by wise men
Yet with no earthly throne.

Jesus,
Son of David
Who came in humble triumph
To show a new way.

Jesus,
Great high priest
Who came to fulfil the law but not to maintain it
Who challenged the make-up of the day in favour of grace.

Jesus,
Friend of sinners
Who befriended the outcast
And healed the sick.

Jesus,
Wonderful Counsellor
Who washed the feet of his disciples
To be a servant to the world.

Jesus,
Bread of life and true vine
Who offered up Himself to feed all people
So that no one should hunger or thirst.

Jesus,
Prince of peace
Who when the crowds shouted "Crucify"
Prayed, "Father forgive."

Jesus,
Lamb of God
Branded as a scapegoat and a sacrifice offered
A ransom paid for us all.

Jesus,
Son of man
Was lain in a borrowed tomb
Quiet and still
Fostering hope and rekindling the flame.

Jesus,
Light of the world
Who overcame the darkness
And ushered in a new dawn.

Jesus,
Name above all names
Promised, ascended and glorified
Lead us on.

# Walking in Jesus' footsteps

Let us walk in the footsteps of Christ.
Let us live His final days with Him again, and let us meet again the man that is God.

Let us ride with Him into the city, and hear the crowds as they hail Him as their king.

Let us eat and drink with Him, and allow him with His words to wash our feet and make us ready for what lies ahead.

Let us go to the garden and wait and pray, as He asked his disciples to do.

Let us stay awake, and witness His betrayal, arrest, trial and crucifixion.

Let us feel His agony and remember it was all for us.

Let us grieve with his friends in the stillness of Saturday.

And let us rejoice in the empty tomb.

Let us ride the rollercoaster of Holy Week with its ups and downs and its twists and turns, knowing and believing that it was all part of God's almighty plan.

**Amen**

# Jesus weeps over Jerusalem
## Palm Sunday:

Matthew 20:1-11
Mark 11:1-11
John 12:12-19.

### Jesus weeps over Jerusalem (Luke 19:41-44)

*[41] As he came near and saw the city, he wept over it, [42] saying, "If you, even you, had only recognized on this day the things that make for peace! But now they are hidden from your eyes. [43] Indeed, the days will come upon you, when your enemies will set up ramparts around you and surround you, and hem you in on every side. [44] They will crush you to the ground, you and your children within you, and they will not leave within you one stone upon another; because you did not recognize the time of your visitation from God."*

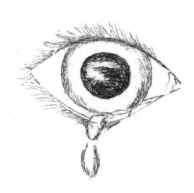

## Jesus weeps over Jerusalem - Luke 19:41-44

Voice 1:    Jesus weeps over Jerusalem, He weeps for a
city lost in pain, darkness and hopelessness.

Voice 2:    We can weep for our cities and communities
that are also lost and without light.

Voice 1:    Jesus weeps over Jerusalem, because the people did not
recognise Him and the unconditional peace and love that He
offered.

Voice 2:    We can weep for our world, that also has been caught up in
violence and hatred and misses all that Christ has to offer.

Voice 1:    Jesus weeps over Jerusalem, He weeps for the city He loved, a
city He prayed for and a city He died for.

Voice 2:    Help us to weep over, and pray with, those around us who
have  not yet seen the light, and have not yet recognised God
in Christ.

Voice 1:    Jesus wept over Jerusalem thousands of years ago, and He is
still weeping.

Voice 2:    Help us to weep with Him for the plight of Jerusalem today.


Amen.

## A day to remember and reflect on
## Maundy Thursday:

Matthew - Chapter 26
Mark - Chapter 14
Luke - Chapter 22
John - Chapter 13

### The Plot to Kill Jesus (Mark 14:1-2)

*"It was two days before the Passover and the festival of Unleavened Bread. The chief priests and the scribes were looking for a way to arrest Jesus by stealth and kill him; [2] for they said, "Not during the festival, or there may be a riot among the people."*

### Judas Agrees to Betray Jesus (Mark 14:10-11)

*"Then Judas Iscariot, who was one of the twelve, went to the chief priests in order to betray him to them. [11] When they heard it, they were greatly pleased, and promised to give him money. So he began to look for an opportunity to betray him."*

### The Institution of the Lord's Supper (Mark 14:22-25)

*"While they were eating, he took a loaf of bread, and after blessing it he broke it, gave it to them, and said, "Take; this is my body." [23] Then he took a cup, and after giving thanks he gave it to them, and all of them drank from it. [24] He said to them, "This is my blood of the covenant, which is poured out for many. [25] Truly I tell you, I will never again drink of the fruit of the vine until that day when I drink it new in the kingdom of God."*

## A day to remember and reflect upon

Leader: Judas agreed to betray Jesus.
All: **May we stand firm against temptation and not give in to betrayal.**

Leader: The disciples shared the Passover with Jesus, His final meal.
All: **Help us to share with each other and the world the food we have. There is enough to go around if distribution is done fairly. Lead us to stand for fair trade and support those who seek to abolish hunger.**

Leader: Jesus took bread and wine and declared them to be for us His body and blood.
All: **As we receive them may we remember that you died for all, and not just those that look or sound like us.**

Leader: In the garden His friends fell asleep and allowed Him to face His anguish alone.
All: **Help us to stay awake, to fight sleep and be alert to the pains of Christ and the world.**

Leader: Judas betrayed Him with a kiss.
All: **Help us to use touch for kindness and healing and not for betrayal and death.**

Leader: Peter denied He even knew Jesus.
All: **Give us the courage to stand up and be counted for Christ whatever that cost might be.**

| | |
|---|---|
| Leader: | The silver, the power, the fame |
| **All:** | **We will reject it** |
| | |
| Leader: | The bread and wine |
| **All:** | **We will share it** |
| | |
| Leader: | The tiredness and apathy |
| **All:** | **We will fight it** |
| | |
| Leader: | The cost |
| **All:** | **We will count it** |
| | |
| Leader: | The cross |
| **All:** | **We will carry it** |
| | |
| Leader: | The resurrection |
| **All:** | **We will live it** |
| | |
| Leader: | The Good News |
| **All:** | **We will impart it to all people** |

**Amen.**

## Jesus shows us how
## Good Friday

Matthew: - Chapter 27     Mark - Chapter 15
Luke - Chapter 23     John - Chapter 19

### The Crucifixion of Jesus (Matthew 27:32-35 / 38-43)

"*As they went out, they came upon a man from Cyrene named Simon; they compelled this man to carry his cross. [33] And when they came to a place called Golgotha (which means Place of a Skull), [34] they offered him wine to drink, mixed with gall; but when he tasted it, he would not drink it. [35] And when they had crucified him, they divided his clothes among themselves by casting lots. [38] Then two bandits were crucified with him, one on his right and one on his left. [39] Those who passed by derided him, shaking their heads [40] and saying, "You who would destroy the temple and build it in three days, save yourself! If you are the Son of God, come down from the cross." [41] In the same way the chief priests also, along with the scribes and elders, were mocking him, saying, [42] "He saved others; he cannot save himself. He is the King of Israel; let him come down from the cross now, and we will believe in him. [43] He trusts in God; let God deliver him now, if he wants to; for he said, 'I am God's Son.' [44] The bandits who were crucified with him also taunted him in the same way.*"

### The Death of Jesus (Matthew 27:45-47)

"*From noon on, darkness came over the whole land until three in the afternoon. [46] And about three o'clock Jesus cried with a loud voice, "Eli, Eli, lema sabachthani?" that is, "My God, my God, why have you forsaken me?" [47] When some of the bystanders heard it, they said, "This man is calling for Elijah."*"

# Jesus shows us how

Voice 1:  His cross was carried by a stranger
Voice 2:  Will we help those strangers among us?
Voice 3:  Jesus shows us how.


Voice 1:  Jesus was crucified between two criminals, who ridiculed Him.
Voice 2:  He offered hope.  Can we offer hope to those that ridicule us?
Voice 3:  Jesus shows us how.


Voice 1:  When Jesus died, darkness covered the earth.
Voice 2:  Today we live in a world that appears to be covered in darkness.  Can we be a light?
Voice 3:  Jesus shows us how.


Voice 1:  When Jesus died, the curtain was torn from top to bottom.
Voice 2:  This gave access to God.  How can we have that too?
Voice 3:  Jesus shows us how.


Voice 1:  When Jesus died He cried out to His Father and felt the pain of separation from His side.
Voice 2:  Many feel the pain of separation.  How can we bridge the gap?
Voice 3:  Jesus shows us how.


Voice 1:  When Jesus died, the priests felt justified.
Voice 2:  When we make bad decisions, and try to justify them, can we be forgiven?
Voice 3:  Jesus shows us how.

Voice 1: When Jesus died soldiers played dice for his clothes.
Voice 2: When we gamble with our lives and the lives of others, can we start again?
Voice 3: Jesus shows us how.

Voice 1: When Jesus died a centurion felt the earth quake and recognised Him for who He really was - the Son of God.
Voice 2: Can we open our eyes to see the real Jesus, and show Him to others?
Voice 3: Jesus shows us how.

Voice 1: When Jesus died women stood and looked on.
Voice 2: Today there are many onlookers. Can we enfold them and help them to join the journey into light?
Voice 3: Jesus shows us how.

**All: When Jesus died**
**He gave us life.**

# In the stillness of silence
## Holy Saturday

Matthew 27:57-66
Mark 15:42-47
Luke 23:50-56
John 19:38-42

### The Burial of Jesus (Luke 23:50-56)

*"Now there was a good and righteous man named Joseph, who, though a member of the council, [51] had not agreed to their plan and action. He came from the Jewish town of Arimathea, and he was waiting expectantly for the kingdom of God. [52] This man went to Pilate and asked for the body of Jesus. [53] Then he took it down, wrapped it in a linen cloth, and laid it in a rock-hewn tomb where no one had ever been laid. [54] It was the day of Preparation, and the Sabbath was beginning. [55] The women who had come with him from Galilee followed, and they saw the tomb and how his body was laid. [56] Then they returned, and prepared spices and ointments.*

*On the Sabbath they rested according to the commandment."*

# In the stillness of silence

In the stillness of silence
A borrowed tomb became His resting place.

In the stillness of silence
A stone was rolled across the entrance.

In the stillness of silence
His friends grieved in an upper room.

In the stillness of silence
The women prepared herbs and spices for burial.

In the stillness of silence
The scribes and priests tasted a hollow victory.

In the stillness of silence
The Roman soldiers believed they had hushed the storm.

In the stillness of silence
Hope appeared lost.

In the stillness of silence
The fire embers gently glowed.

In the stillness of silence
Love prepared to break out.

In the stillness of silence
A new world waited to dawn.

# Called By Name
## Easter Sunday

Matthew - Chapter 28
Mark - Chapter 16
Luke - Chapter 24
John - Chapter 20

### Jesus Appears to Mary Magdalene

*"But Mary stood weeping outside the tomb. As she wept, she bent over to look into the tomb; [12] and she saw two angels in white, sitting where the body of Jesus had been lying, one at the head and the other at the feet. [13] They said to her, "Woman, why are you weeping?" She said to them, "They have taken away my Lord, and I do not know where they have laid him." [14] When she had said this, she turned around and saw Jesus standing there, but she did not know that it was Jesus. [15] Jesus said to her, "Woman, why are you weeping? Whom are you looking for?" Supposing him to be the gardener, she said to him, "Sir, if you have carried him away, tell me where you have laid him, and I will take him away." [16] Jesus said to her, "Mary!" She turned and said to him in Hebrew, "Rabbouni!" (which means Teacher). [17] Jesus said to her, "Do not hold on to me, because I have not yet ascended to the Father. But go to my brothers and say to them, 'I am ascending to my Father and your Father, to my God and your God.'" [18] Mary Magdalene went and announced to the disciples, "I have seen the Lord"; and she told them that he had said these things to her."*

# Called By Name

Called by name.
What does that mean?
What did that mean for Mary?
What does it mean for my world, my community,
For myself?

I heard it once,
My name uttered from a distance
But over the years your voice has grown dim,
Or maybe my ears have just stopped listening.

Called by name.
Call again Lord,
Call, shout, and make me listen,
I want so much to hear you.

Help me to react, respond and be revived.
Help me to live again, to be reborn.
To be renewed.
Ready and willing to go and stand for you.

Called by name.
My name  -  God's call.

# The light has dawned

Hallelujah the light has dawned
The darkness is no more
And death has been defeated.

Hallelujah the light has dawned
The fire has been rekindled
And hope lives again.

Hallelujah the light has dawned
Jesus has broken the spell
The world is free.

Hallelujah the light has dawned
This is a new beginning
The old order has been overturned.

Hallelujah the light has dawned
Nothing can ever be the same again
It is time for change.

Hallelujah the light has dawned
Let us embrace the light that is Christ
And share it with all people.

# In all things  -  Christ is!

In life and death
Christ is.

In hope and despair
Christ is.

In joy and sorrow
Christ is.

Over powers and dominions,
Over government and finance,
Over human theologies,
Over broken dreams,
Christ is.

When death came
It could not hold Him.

When mourning came
It could not last.

When darkness came
The light was not far behind.

In life and death
Christ is.

In all things in heaven and on earth
Christ is.

## With the rising sun

Dear Lord,

Early in the morning we stand and watch the sun rise.
We greet it with joy and song and prayer,
But the sun always rises
Yet today, Your Son has risen.

We remember His last meal with His friends
His betrayal
Those that denied and scattered.
We remember a mock trial,
A paid-off court room
And an undeserved death sentence.
But today, He has risen.

We remember the pain of the cross,
The agony of death,
The moment of separation from You that Christ suffered.
And we remember that He endured it all, for us.
But today, He has risen.

Today Jesus walks among the living,
Today grave clothes are no longer needed,
Today new life has sprung,
Today He has risen,
And hope has risen with Him.
So let us put our trust in Him
For once he was dead
And now He is risen.

Amen

## Blessing

Today and tomorrow we travel with Jesus
**Help us to be good companions.**

Today and tomorrow we are called to be his hands and feet.
**Help us to follow His example.**

Today and tomorrow we are asked to shine a light in the darkness.
**Help us to draw strength from the beacon that is Christ.**

Today and tomorrow we are asked to provide for the hungry and thirsty.
**Help us to remember that Jesus offers life-giving water that will
never run dry.**

Today and tomorrow we are sustained by God
**Father, Son and Holy Spirit.**


**Amen.**

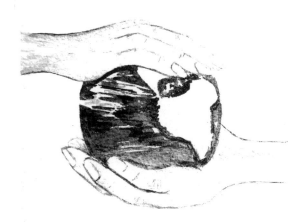

### <u>Do not worry</u>

*<sup>28</sup> And why do you worry about clothing? Consider the lilies of the field, how they grow; they neither toil nor spin, <sup>29</sup> yet I tell you, even Solomon in all his glory was not clothed like one of these. <sup>30</sup> But if God so clothes the grass of the field, which is alive today and tomorrow is thrown into the oven, will he not much more clothe you—you of little faith? <sup>31</sup> Therefore do not worry, saying, 'What will we eat?' or 'What will we drink?' or 'What will we wear?' <sup>32</sup> For it is the Gentiles who strive for all these things; and indeed your heavenly Father knows that you need all these things. <sup>33</sup> But strive first for the kingdom of God and his righteousness, and all these things will be given to you as well.*

*<sup>34</sup> "So do not worry about tomorrow, for tomorrow will bring worries of its own. Today's trouble is enough for today."*

*Matthew 6:28-34*

## Blessed be - Matthew 5: 3-11

*3 "Blessed are the poor in spirit, for theirs is the kingdom of heaven.*
*4 "Blessed are those who mourn, for they will be comforted.*
*5 "Blessed are the meek, for they will inherit the earth.*
*6 "Blessed are those who hunger and thirst for righteousness, for they*
*will be filled.*
*7 "Blessed are the merciful, for they will receive mercy.*
*8 "Blessed are the pure in heart, for they will see God.*
*9 "Blessed are the peacemakers, for they will be called children of God.*
*10 "Blessed are those who are persecuted for righteousness' sake, for*
*theirs is the kingdom of heaven.*

*11 "Blessed are you when people revile you and persecute you and utter*
*all kinds of evil against you falsely on my account. 12 Rejoice and be*
*glad, for your reward is great in heaven, for in the same way they*
*persecuted the prophets who were before you."*